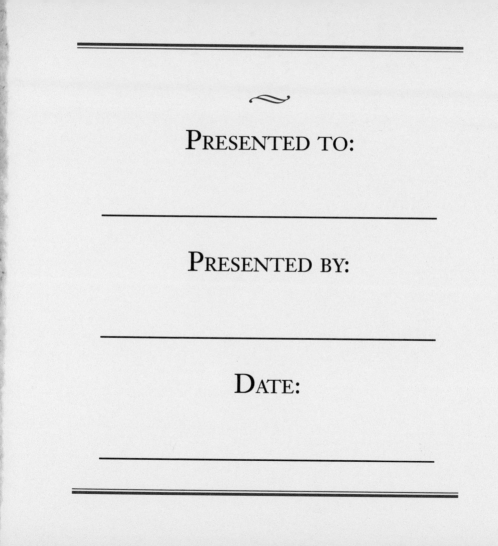

PRESENTED TO:

_____

PRESENTED BY:

_____

DATE:

_____

GOD'S LITTLE INSTRUCTION BOOK
FOR MEN
—SPECIAL GIFT EDITION

HONOR
BOOKS

Tulsa, Oklahoma

God's Little Instruction Book for Men—Special Gift Edition
ISBN 1-56292-263-7
Copyright © 1997 by Honor Books, Inc.
P. O. Box 55388
Tulsa, Oklahoma 74155

INTRODUCTION

God's Little Instruction Book for Men—Special Gift Edition, is a power-packed inspirational collection of dynamic quotes, which are coupled with the wisdom of the ages, God's Word. They will motivate men of all faiths and vocations to live a meaningful, productive, and happy life, while inspiring them to strive for excellence and character in living.

This book is designed to be fun to read, yet thought-provoking, supplying men with godly insight on many topics vital to life. Within these pages are familiar and unfamiliar quotes covering subjects such as personal achievement, excellence, integrity, and how to find real success in life. An inspirational verse is included after each quote, so as to include what the instruction manual of life, the Bible, has to say about each topic.

God's Little Instruction Book for Men—Special Gift Edition will challenge men to move beyond the status quo of society and develop a vision for themselves to become the men God created them to be.

WHEN GOD MEASURES A MAN, HE PUTS THE TAPE AROUND THE HEART INSTEAD OF THE HEAD.

~

For the Lord seeth not as man seeth;
for man looketh on the outward appearance,
but the Lord looketh on the heart.
1 Samuel 16:7

THE WAY EACH DAY WILL LOOK TO YOU ALL STARTS WITH WHO YOU'RE LOOKING TO.

*I will lift up mine eyes unto the hills,
from whence cometh my help. My help cometh
from the Lord, which made heaven and earth.*
Psalm 121:1,2

LIVE TRUTH INSTEAD OF PROFESSING IT.

~

But be ye doers of the word,
and not hearers only, deceiving your own selves.
James 1:22

IMPOSSIBILITIES VANISH WHEN A MAN AND HIS GOD CONFRONT A MOUNTAIN.

~

...but with God all things are possible.
Matthew 19:26

WE TOO OFTEN LOVE THINGS AND USE PEOPLE, WHEN WE SHOULD BE USING THINGS AND LOVING PEOPLE.

~

Be devoted to one another in brotherly love.
Honor one another above yourselves.
Romans 12:10 NIV

HONOR

IS BETTER

THAN HONORS.

~

...for them that honour me I will honour.
1 Samuel 2:30

IT IS NOT WHAT A MAN DOES THAT DETERMINES WHETHER HIS WORK IS SACRED OR SECULAR, IT IS WHY HE DOES IT.

Whatever you do, work at it with all your heart,
as working for the Lord, not for men....
It is the Lord Christ you are serving.
Colossians 3:23,24 NIV

CHARACTER

IS WHAT YOU ARE

IN THE DARK.

~

The integrity of the upright shall guide them.
Proverbs 11:3

THE ULTIMATE MEASURE OF A
MAN IS NOT WHERE HE STANDS
IN MOMENTS OF COMFORT AND
CONVENIENCE, BUT WHERE
HE STANDS AT TIMES OF
CHALLENGE AND CONTROVERSY.

If thou faint in the day of adversity,
thy strength is small.
Proverbs 24:10

IF YOU TELL THE TRUTH, YOU DON'T HAVE TO REMEMBER ANYTHING.

~

A truthful witness gives honest testimony,
but a false witness tells lies.
Proverbs 12:17 NIV

TRUST IN YOURSELF AND YOU ARE
DOOMED TO DISAPPOINTMENT...
TRUST IN MONEY AND YOU MAY HAVE
IT TAKEN FROM YOU...BUT TRUST
IN GOD, AND YOU ARE NEVER TO BE
CONFOUNDED IN TIME OR ETERNITY.

It is better to take refuge in the Lord
than to trust in man.
Psalm 118:8 NIV

THE SUPERIOR MAN... STANDS ERECT BY BENDING ABOVE THE FALLEN. HE RISES BY LIFTING OTHERS.

~

And we urge you, brethren, admonish the unruly,
encourage the fainthearted, help the weak,
be patient with all men.
1 Thessalonians 5:14 NASB

YOU CAN'T DO MUCH ABOUT YOUR ANCESTORS, BUT YOU CAN INFLUENCE YOUR DESCENDANTS ENORMOUSLY.

...but as for me and my house, we will serve the Lord.
Joshua 24:15

THE STRONGEST EVIDENCE OF LOVE IS SACRIFICE.

~

For God so loved the world,
that he gave his only begotten Son,
that whosoever believeth in him
should not perish, but have everlasting life.
John 3:16

THE MAN WHO FEARS NO TRUTHS HAS NOTHING TO FEAR FROM LIES.

~

May your love and your truth always protect me.
Psalm 40:11 NIV

MEN WILL SPEND THEIR HEALTH GETTING WEALTH; THEN GLADLY PAY ALL THEY HAVE EARNED TO GET HEALTH BACK.

∽

*People who want to get rich fall into temptation and a trap
and into many foolish and harmful desires
that plunge men into ruin and destruction.*
I Timothy 6:9 NIV

THE FIRST DUTY OF LOVE IS TO LISTEN.

~

Wherfore, my beloved brethren,
let every man be swift to hear.
James 1:19

No person was ever honored for what he received. Honor has been the reward for what he gave.

~

The righteous giveth and spareth not.
Proverbs 21:26

RESPONSIBILITY IS THE THING PEOPLE DREAD MOST OF ALL. YET IT IS THE ONE THING IN THE WORLD THAT DEVELOPS US, GIVES US MANHOOD...FIBER.

~

Blessed is that servant,
whom his lord when he cometh shall find so doing.
Luke 12:43

PERHAPS ONCE IN A HUNDRED YEARS A PERSON MAY BE RUINED BY EXCESSIVE PRAISE, BUT SURELY ONCE EVERY MINUTE SOMEONE DIES INSIDE FOR LACK OF IT.

~

Let no corrupt communication proceed out of your mouth, but that which is good to the use of edifying, that it may minister grace unto the hearers.
Ephesians 4:29

BIG PEOPLE MONOPOLIZE THE LISTENING. SMALL PEOPLE MONOPOLIZE THE TALKING.

~

Seest thou a man that is hasty in his words?
there is more hope of a fool than of him.
Proverbs 29:20

GOD SENDS NO ONE AWAY EXCEPT THOSE WHO ARE FULL OF THEMSELVES.

~

God resisteth the proud, and giveth grace to the humble.
1 Peter 5:5

THE MEASURE OF A MAN IS NOT WHAT HE DOES ON SUNDAY, BUT RATHER WHO HE IS MONDAY THROUGH SATURDAY.

~

...that you may live worthy of the Lord and may please him in every way: bearing fruit in every good work.
Colossians 1:10 NIV

THE WORLD IS BLESSED MOST BY MEN WHO DO THINGS, AND NOT BY THOSE WHO MERELY TALK ABOUT THEM.

~

But be ye doers of the word, and not hearers only,
deceiving your own selves.
James 1:22

AUTHORITY
WITHOUT WISDOM
IS LIKE A HEAVY AX
WITHOUT AN EDGE,
FITTER TO BRUISE
THAN POLISH.

~

...the authority the Lord gave us
for building you up, not for tearing you down.
2 Corinthians 13:10 NIV

THE BEST WAY TO TEACH CHARACTER IS TO HAVE IT AROUND THE HOUSE.

~

A righteous man who walks in integrity —
How blessed are his sons after him.
Proverbs 20:7 NASB

THE MAN WHO WINS MAY HAVE BEEN COUNTED OUT SEVERAL TIMES, BUT HE DIDN'T HEAR THE REFEREE.

~

Though a righteous man falls seven times, he rises again.
Proverbs 24:16 NIV

IT IS IMPOSSIBLE FOR THAT MAN TO DESPAIR WHO REMEMBERS THAT HIS HELPER IS OMNIPOTENT.

~

I will lift up my eyes to the mountains;
from whence shall my help come? My help comes
from the Lord, Who made heaven and earth.
Psalm 121:1,2 NASB

IF THERE BE ANY TRUER MEASURE OF A MAN THAN BY WHAT HE DOES, IT MUST BE BY WHAT HE GIVES.

~

It is more blessed to give than to receive.
Acts 20:35

MEN
FOR THE SAKE
OF GETTING A LIVING
FORGET TO LIVE.

~

It is vain for you to rise up early, to take rest late,
to eat the bread of [anxious] toil —
for He gives [blessings] to His beloved [in sleep.]
Psalm 127:2 AMP

IF A MAN CANNOT BE A CHRISTIAN IN THE PLACE WHERE HE IS, HE CANNOT BE A CHRISTIAN ANYWHERE.

~

Let your light so shine before men, that they may see your good works, and glorify your Father which is in heaven.
Matthew 5:16

YOU CANNOT LIVE A PERFECT DAY WITHOUT DOING SOMETHING FOR SOMEONE WHO WILL NEVER BE ABLE TO REPAY YOU.

~

And do not forget to do good and to share with others,
for with such sacrifices God is pleased.
Hebrews 13:16 NIV

EVERY MAN IS ENTHUSIASTIC AT TIMES. ONE MAN HAS ENTHUSIASM FOR THIRTY MINUTES, ANOTHER HAS IT FOR THIRTY DAYS — BUT IT IS THE MAN WHO HAS IT FOR THIRTY YEARS WHO MAKES A SUCCESS IN LIFE.

~

Let us run with perserverance the race marked out for us.
Hebrews 12:1 NIV

MEASURE WEALTH NOT BY THE THINGS YOU HAVE, BUT BY THE THINGS YOU HAVE FOR WHICH YOU WOULD NOT TAKE MONEY.

~

A man's life consisteth not in the abundance
of the things which he possesseth.
Luke 12:15

THE FOOLISH MAN SEEKS HAPPINESS IN THE DISTANCE; THE WISE GROWS IT UNDER HIS FEET.

~

I have learned, in whatsoever state I am,
therewith to be content.
Philippians 4:11

SEEK GOD FIRST AND THE THINGS YOU WANT WILL SEEK YOU.

~

But seek ye first the kingdom of God, and his righteousness;
and all these things shall be added unto you.
Matthew 6:33

THE STRENGTH OF A MAN CONSISTS IN FINDING OUT THE WAY GOD IS GOING, AND GOING THAT WAY.

~

I am the light of the world: he that followeth me shall not walk in darkness, but shall have the light of life.
John 8:12

UNTIL YOU MAKE PEACE WITH WHO YOU ARE, YOU'LL NEVER BE CONTENT WITH WHAT YOU HAVE.

~

But godliness with contentment is great gain.
1 Timothy 6:6

A GENTLEMAN

IS

A GENTLE MAN.

And the servant of the Lord must not strive;
but be gentle unto all men.
2 Timothy 2:24

(THE CALLED MAN) SEES HIMSELF AS A STEWARD...HE'S OBEDIENT RATHER THAN AMBITIOUS, COMMITTED RATHER THAN COMPETITIVE. FOR HIM, NOTHING IS MORE IMPORTANT THAN PLEASING THE ONE WHO CALLED HIM.

~

We obey his commands and do what pleases him.
1 John 3:22 NIV

IF I TAKE CARE OF MY CHARACTER, MY REPUTATION WILL TAKE CARE OF ITSELF.

~

Righteousness guards the man of integrity.
Proverbs 13:6 NIV

MANY RECEIVE ADVICE, ONLY THE WISE PROFIT BY IT.

~

Pride only breeds quarrels,
but wisdom is found in those who take advice.
Proverbs 13:10 NIV

I HAVE NEVER BEEN HURT BY ANYTHING I DIDN'T SAY.

~

*Don't talk so much. You keep putting your foot
in your mouth. Be sensible and turn off the flow!*
Proverbs 10:19 TLB

SUCCESS IS KNOWING THE DIFFERENCE BETWEEN CORNERING PEOPLE AND GETTING THEM IN YOUR CORNER.

~

Can two walk together, except they be agreed?
Amos 3:3

NO HORSE GETS ANYWHERE UNTIL HE IS HARNESSED. NO LIFE EVER GROWS GREAT UNTIL IT IS FOCUSED, DEDICATED, DISCIPLINED.

~

In a race, everyone runs but only one person gets first prize.... To win the contest you must deny yourselves many things that would keep you from doing your best.
1 Corinthians 9:24,25 TLB

THE WAY TO GET TO THE TOP IS TO GET OFF YOUR BOTTOM.

~

How long will you lie down, O sluggard?
When will you arise from your sleep?
Proverbs 6:9 NASB

THERE ARE TIMES WHEN SILENCE IS GOLDEN; OTHER TIMES IT IS JUST PLAIN YELLOW.

To every thing there is a season...
a time to keep silence, and a time to speak.
Ecclesiastes 3:1,7

EVERY JOB IS A SELF-PORTRAIT OF THE PERSON WHO DOES IT. AUTOGRAPH YOUR WORK WITH EXCELLENCE.

∽

Daniel was preferred above the presidents and princes,
because an excellent spirit was in him.
Daniel 6:3

THE BEST THINGS IN LIFE ARE NOT FREE.

~

Forasmuch as ye know that ye were not redeemed
with corruptible things, as silver and gold....
But with the precious blood of Christ,
as of a lamb without blemish and without spot.
1 Peter 1:18,19

DON'T ASK GOD FOR WHAT YOU THINK IS GOOD; ASK HIM FOR WHAT HE THINKS IS GOOD FOR YOU.

After this manner therefore pray ye.... Thy kingdom come.
Thy will be done in earth, as it is in heaven.
Matthew 6:9,10

DON'T BE DISCOURAGED; EVERYONE WHO GOT WHERE HE IS, STARTED WHERE HE WAS.

~

Though your beginning was insignificant,
Yet your end will increase greatly.
Job 8:7 NASB

MATURITY DOESN'T COME WITH AGE; IT COMES WITH ACCEPTANCE OF RESPONSIBILITY.

~

When I was a child, I spake as a child,
I understood as a child, I thought as a child:
but when I became a man, I put away childish things.
1 Corinthians 13:11

THE HAPPIEST PEOPLE DON'T NECESSARILY HAVE THE BEST OF EVERYTHING. THEY JUST MAKE THE BEST OF EVERYTHING.

~

For I have learned, in whatsoever state I am, therewith to be content. I can do all things hrough Christ which strengtheneth me.
Philippians 4:11,13

LEARN
BY EXPERIENCE —
PREFERABLY
OTHER PEOPLE'S.

~

All these things happened to them as examples — as object lessons to us — to warn us against doing the same things.
1 Corinthians 10:11 TLB

IT'S NOT HARD TO MAKE DECISIONS WHEN YOU KNOW WHAT YOUR VALUES ARE.

*But Daniel purposed in his heart
that he would not defile himself.
Daniel 1:8*

THE END MUST JUSTIFY THE MEANS.

~

The just man walketh in his integrity:
his children are blessed after him.
Proverbs 20:7

ADVERSITY CAUSES SOME MEN TO BREAK; OTHERS TO BREAK RECORDS.

~

If thou faint in the day of adversity, thy strength is small.
Proverbs 24:10

A MAN WHO WANTS TO LEAD THE ORCHESTRA MUST TURN HIS BACK ON THE CROWD.

~

Wherefore come out from among them,
and be ye separate, saith the Lord.
2 Corinthians 6:17

MEN ARE ALIKE IN THEIR PROMISES. IT IS ONLY IN THEIR DEEDS THAT THEY DIFFER.

~

Many a man claims to have unfailing love,
but a faithful man who can find?
Proverbs 20:6 NIV

CONQUER YOURSELF

RATHER THAN THE WORLD.

~

Similarly, encourage the young men to be self-controlled.
Titus 2:6 NIV

HE WHO HAS LEARNED TO OBEY WILL KNOW HOW TO COMMAND.

~

The wise in heart accept commands,
but a chattering fool comes to ruin.
Proverbs 10:8 NIV

YOU MUST HAVE LONG-RANGE GOALS TO KEEP YOU FROM BEING FRUSTRATED BY SHORT-RANGE FAILURES.

~

Let us fix our eyes on Jesus, the author and perfecter
of our faith, who for the joy set before him
endured the cross, scorning its shame,
and sat down at the right hand of the throne of God.
Hebrews 12:2 NIV

THE FUTURE BELONGS TO THOSE WHO BELIEVE IN THE BEAUTY OF THEIR DREAMS.

~

Anything is possible if you have faith.
Mark 9:23 TLB

THE FUTURE BELONGS TO THOSE WHO SEE POSSIBILITIES BEFORE THEY BECOME OBVIOUS.

For the vision is yet for an appointed time...
it will surely come, it will not tarry.
Habakkuk 2:3

PERSERVERANCE IS A GREAT ELEMENT OF SUCCESS; IF YOU ONLY KNOCK LONG ENOUGH AND LOUD ENOUGH AT THE GATE, YOU ARE SURE TO WAKE UP SOMEBODY.

~

Ask, and it shall be given you; seek, and ye shall find;
knock, and it shall be opened unto you.
Luke 11:9

THE MOST VALUABLE OF ALL TALENTS IS THAT OF NEVER USING TWO WORDS WHEN ONE WILL DO.

~

In the multitude of words there wanteth not sin:
but he that refraineth his lips is wise.
Proverbs 10:19

NOTHING GREAT WAS EVER ACHIEVED WITHOUT ENTHUSIASM.

...for the joy of the Lord is your strength.
Nehemiah 8:10

CARVE YOUR NAME

ON HEARTS

AND NOT ON MARBLE.

~

The only letter I need is you yourselves!
They can see that you are a letter from Christ, written
by us...not one carved on stone,
but in human hearts.
2 Corinthians 3:2,3 TLB

ONE-HALF
THE TROUBLE OF THIS LIFE
CAN BE TRACED TO SAYING
YES TOO QUICK, AND NOT
SAYING NO SOON ENOUGH.

~

Seest thou a man that is hasty in his words?
there is more hope of a fool than of him.
Proverbs 29:20

YOU CAN ACCOMPLISH MORE IN ONE HOUR WITH GOD THAN ONE LIFETIME WITHOUT HIM.

~

With God all things are possible.
Matthew 19:26

MAN CANNOT DISCOVER NEW OCEANS UNLESS HE HAS THE COURAGE TO LOSE SIGHT OF THE SHORE.

~

Peter got out of the boat,
and walked on the water and came toward Jesus.
Matthew 14:29 NASB

"THE SUPERVISOR'S PRAYER"

LORD WHEN I AM WRONG, MAKE ME WILLING TO CHANGE; WHEN I AM RIGHT, MAKE ME EASY TO LIVE WITH. SO STRENGTHEN ME THAT THE POWER OF MY EXAMPLE WILL FAR EXCEED THE AUTHORITY OF MY RANK.

*...to offer ourselves as a model for you,
that you might follow our example.*
2 Thessalonians 3:9 NASB

ONE MAN WITH COURAGE

MAKES A MAJORITY.

*Be strong and of a good courage...for the Lord thy God
...will not fail thee, nor forsake thee.*
Deuteronomy 31:6

A MAN NEVER DISCLOSES HIS OWN CHARACTER SO CLEARLY AS WHEN HE DESCRIBES ANOTHER'S.

A good man out of the good treasure of the heart
bringeth forth good things: and an evil man
out of the evil treasure bringeth forth evil things.
Matthew 12:35

THE GREATEST USE OF LIFE IS TO SPEND IT FOR SOMETHING THAT WILL OUTLAST IT.

~

But store up for yourselves treasures in heaven,
where moth and rust do not destroy,
and where thieves do not break in and steal.
Matthew 6:20 NIV

WHAT WE DO ON SOME GREAT OCCASION WILL PROBABLY DEPEND ON WHAT WE ALREADY ARE; AND WHAT WE ARE WILL BE THE RESULT OF PREVIOUS YEARS OF SELF-DISCIPLINE.

~

But I keep under my body, and bring it into subjection.
1 Corinthians 9:27

OUR DEEDS DETERMINE US, AS MUCH AS WE DETERMINE OUR DEEDS.

~

Even a child is known by his actions,
by whether his conduct is pure and right.
Proverbs 20:11 NIV

NO MATTER WHAT A MAN'S PAST MAY HAVE BEEN, HIS FUTURE IS SPOTLESS.

~

...forgetting those things which are behind and reaching forth unto those things which are before.
Philippians 3:13

EVERYTHING COMES TO HIM WHO HUSTLES WHILE HE WAITS.

~

We do not want you to become lazy,
but to imitate those who through faith
and patience inherit what has been promised.
Hebrews 6:12 NIV

DEFEAT IS NOT THE WORST OF FAILURES. NOT TO HAVE TRIED IS THE TRUE FAILURE.

~

Be strong and of a good courage; be not afraid, neither be thou dismayed: for the Lord thy God is with thee whithersoever thou goest.
Joshua 1:9

I WOULD RATHER FAIL IN THE CAUSE THAT SOMEDAY WILL TRIUMPH THAN TRIUMPH IN A CAUSE THAT SOMEDAY WILL FAIL.

∽

Now thanks be unto God,
which always causeth us to triumph in Christ.
2 Corinthians 2:14

THE SECRET OF SUCCESS IS TO BE LIKE A DUCK — SMOOTH AND UNRUFFLED ON TOP, BUT PADDLING FURIOUSLY UNDERNEATH.

~

I laboured more abundantly than they all: yet not I,
but the grace of God which was with me.
1 Corinthians 15:10

No plan is worth the paper it is printed on unless it starts you doing something.

~

But be ye doers of the word,
and not hearers only, deceiving your own selves.
James 1:22

LIFE IS A COIN.
YOU CAN SPEND IT
ANY WAY YOU WISH,
BUT YOU CAN SPEND IT
ONLY ONCE.

~

He that is greatest among you shall be your servant...
and he that shall humble himself shall be exalted.
Matthew 23:11,12

ONLY PASSIONS, GREAT PASSIONS, CAN ELEVATE THE SOUL TO GREAT THINGS.

~

...fervent in spirit; serving the Lord.
Romans 12:11

FAILURES WANT PLEASING METHODS, SUCCESSES WANT PLEASING RESULTS.

~

No discipline seems pleasant at the time, but painful.
Later on, however, it produces a harvest of righteousness
and peace for those who have been trained by it.
Hebrews 12:11 NIV

MOST OF THE THINGS WORTH DOING IN THE WORLD HAD BEEN DECLARED IMPOSSIBLE BEFORE THEY WERE DONE.

~

With God all things are possible.
Matthew 19:26

A GOOD REPUTATION IS MORE VALUABLE THAN MONEY.

~

A good name is rather to be chosen than great riches.
Proverbs 22:1

THE WORLD BELONGS TO THE MAN WHO IS WISE ENOUGH TO CHANGE HIS MIND IN THE PRESENCE OF FACTS.

~

Whoever heeds correction gains understanding.
Proverbs 15:32 NIV

EVERY CALLING IS GREAT WHEN GREATLY PURSUED.

~

*I press toward the mark for the prize
of the high calling of God in Christ Jesus.*
Philippians 3:14

PATIENCE
IS BITTER
BUT ITS FRUIT
IS SWEET.

~

For ye have need of patience, that, after ye have done
the will of God, ye might receive the promise.
Hebrews 10:36

GENTLEMEN,
TRY NOT TO BECOME
MEN OF SUCCESS.
RATHER, BECOME
MEN OF VALUE.

~

The just man walketh in his integrity.
Proverbs 20:7

WHEN YOU ARE LABORING FOR OTHERS LET IT BE WITH THE SAME ZEAL AS IF IT WERE FOR YOURSELF.

~

Each of you should look not only to your own interests,
but also to the interests of others.
Philippians 2:4 NIV

MONEY

IS A GOOD SERVANT

BUT A BAD MASTER.

The rich ruleth over the poor,
and the borrower is servant to the lender.
Proverbs 22:7

WHEN YOU DO THE THINGS YOU HAVE TO DO WHEN YOU HAVE TO DO THEM, THE DAY WILL COME WHEN YOU CAN DO THE THINGS YOU WANT TO DO WHEN YOU WANT TO DO THEM.

~

He becometh poor that dealeth with a slack hand:
but the hand of the diligent maketh rich.
Proverbs 10:4

THE TWO MOST IMPORTANT WORDS: "THANK YOU." THE MOST IMPORTANT WORD: "WE." THE LEAST IMPORTANT WORD: "I."

~

Don't be selfish....Be humble,
thinking of others as better than yourself.
Philippians 2:3 TLB

I COUNT HIM BRAVER WHO OVERCOMES HIS DESIRES THAN HIM WHO CONQUERS HIS ENEMIES; FOR THE HARDEST VICTORY IS THE VICTORY OVER SELF.

~

But I keep under my body; and bring it into subjection.
1 Corinthians 9:27

COURAGE IS RESISTANCE TO FEAR, MASTERY OF FEAR — NOT ABSENCE OF FEAR.

~

Yea, though I walk through the valley of the shadow of death, I will fear no evil: for thou art with me; thy rod and thy staff they comfort me.
Psalm 23:4

LET US NOT SAY, EVERY MAN IS THE ARCHITECT OF HIS OWN FORTUNE; BUT LET US SAY, EVERY MAN IS THE ARCHITECT OF HIS OWN CHARACTER.

~

Till I die I will not remove mine integrity from me.
My righteousness I hold fast, and will not let it go:
my heart shall not reproach me so long as I live.
Job 27:5,6

PEOPLE, PLACES, AND THINGS WERE NEVER MEANT TO GIVE US LIFE. GOD ALONE IS THE AUTHOR OF A FULFILLING LIFE.

~

I am come that they might have life,
and that they might have it more abundantly.
John 10:10

THE GREATEST ACT OF FAITH IS WHEN MAN DECIDES HE IS NOT GOD.

~

Know ye that the Lord he is God:
it is he that hath made us, and not we ourselves;
we are his people, and the sheep of his pasture.
Psalm 100:3

A TRUE FRIEND NEVER GETS IN YOUR WAY UNLESS YOU HAPPEN TO BE GOING DOWN.

*A friend loves at all times,
and a brother is born for adversity.
Proverbs 17:17 NASB*

CHARACTER
IS NOT MADE IN CRISIS,
IT IS ONLY EXHIBITED.

I have set the Lord always before me:
because he is at my right hand, I shall not be moved.
Psalm 16:8

WISDOM IS THE QUALITY THAT KEEPS YOU FROM GETTING INTO SITUATIONS WHERE YOU NEED IT.

~

I would have you learn this great fact:
that a life of doing right is the wisest life there is.
If you live that kind of life,
you'll not limp or stumble as you run.
Proverbs 4:11,12 TLB

GOD HAS A HISTORY OF USING THE INSIGNIFICANT TO ACCOMPLISH THE IMPOSSIBLE.

~

And Jesus looking upon them saith,
With men it is impossible, but not with God:
for with God all things are possible.
Mark 10:27

IT'S NOT HOW MANY HOURS YOU PUT IN BUT HOW MUCH YOU PUT INTO THE HOURS.

~

Whatever you do, work at it with all your heart,
as working for the Lord, not for men.
Colossians 3:23 NIV

THE TROUBLE WITH MOST OF US IS THAT WE WOULD RATHER BE RUINED BY PRAISE THAN SAVED BY CRITICISM.

~

If you profit from constructive criticism you will be elected to the wise men's hall of fame. But to reject criticism is to harm yourself and your own best interests.
Proverbs 15:31,32 TLB

FOR PEACE OF MIND, RESIGN AS GENERAL MANAGER OF THE UNIVERSE.

~

Cease striving and know that I am God...
Psalm 46:10 NASB

AN ATHIEST IS A MAN WHO HAS NO INVISIBLE MEANS OF SUPPORT.

~

The fool hath said in his heart, There is no God.
Psalm 53:1

A HALF-TRUTH IS USUALLY LESS THAN HALF OF THAT.

~

The Lord detests lying lips,
but He delights in men who are truthful.
Proverbs 12:22 NIV

AS I GROW OLDER, I PAY LESS ATTENTION TO WHAT MEN SAY. I JUST WATCH WHAT THEY DO.

*Show me your faith without deeds
and I will show you my faith by what I do.*
James 2:18 NIV

SOME PEOPLE REACH THE TOP OF THE LADDER OF SUCCESS ONLY TO FIND IT IS LEANING AGAINST THE WRONG WALL.

~

But seek ye first the kingdom of God, and his righteousness;
and all these things shall be added unto you.
Matthew 6:33

IF YOU WERE GIVEN A NICKNAME DESCRIPTIVE OF YOUR CHARACTER, WOULD YOU BE PROUD OF IT?

~

A good name is rather to be chosen than great riches.
Proverbs 22:1

PRAY AS IF EVERYTHING DEPENDED ON GOD, AND WORK AS IF EVERYTHING DEPENDED UPON MAN.

~

Faith without works is dead.
James 2:26

THE TROUBLE WITH STRETCHING THE TRUTH IS THAT IT'S APT TO SNAP BACK.

~

A false witness shall not be unpunished,
and he that speaketh lies shall not escape.
Proverbs 19:5

A BLIND MAN
WHO SEES
IS BETTER THAN
A SEEING MAN
WHO IS BLIND.

~

But blessed are your eyes, for they see:
and your ears, for they hear.
Matthew 13:16

MEN OCCASIONALLY STUMBLE OVER THE TRUTH, BUT MOST OF THEM PICK THEMSELVES UP AND HURRY OFF AS IF NOTHING HAPPENED.

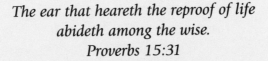

The ear that heareth the reproof of life
abideth among the wise.
Proverbs 15:31

THE WORLD WANTS YOUR BEST BUT GOD WANTS YOUR ALL.

For whosoever will save his life shall lose it;
but whosoever shall lose his life for my sake
and the gospel's, the same shall save it.
Mark 8:35

PERSONALITY HAS THE POWER TO OPEN DOORS, BUT CHARACTER KEEPS THEM OPEN.

~

The righteous shall never be removed.
Proverbs 10:30

ONLY WHEN WE HAVE KNELT BEFORE GOD, CAN WE STAND BEFORE MEN.

~

Humble yoursleves therefore under the mighty hand of God,
that he may exalt you in due time.
1 Peter 5:6

IT IS POSSIBLE TO BE TOO BIG FOR GOD TO USE YOU BUT NEVER TOO SMALL FOR GOD TO USE YOU.

~

A man's pride brings him low,
but a man of lowly spirit gains honor.
Proverbs 29:23 NIV

A CHRISTIAN

MUST KEEP THE FAITH,

BUT NOT TO HIMSELF.

~

Go ye into all the world,
and preach the gospel to every creature.
Mark 16:15

HE WHO PROVIDES FOR THIS LIFE, BUT TAKES NO CARE FOR ETERNITY, IS WISE FOR A MOMENT, BUT A FOOL FOREVER.

*What is a man profited, if he shall gain
the whole world, and lose his own soul?
or what shall a man give in exchange for his soul?
Matthew 16:26*

COURAGE IS CONTAGIOUS. WHEN A BRAVE MAN TAKES A STAND, THE SPINES OF OTHERS ARE STIFFENED.

~

Stand firm in the faith; be men of courage; be strong.
1 Corinthians 16:13 NIV

THE MAN WHO SINGS HIS OWN PRAISES ALWAYS GETS THE WRONG PITCH.

~

Let another man praise thee, and not thine own mouth;
a stranger, and not thine own lips.
Proverbs 27:2

MOTIVATION

IS WHEN YOUR DREAMS

PUT ON WORK CLOTHES.

~

Whatever you do, work at it with all your heart,
as working for the Lord, not for men.
Colossians 3:23 NIV

IF GOD

BE YOUR PARTNER,

MAKE YOUR PLANS LARGE.

~

I can do all things through Christ which strengtheneth me.
Philippians 4:13

WHENEVER A MAN IS READY TO UNCOVER HIS SINS, GOD IS ALWAYS READY TO COVER THEM.

~

He that covereth his sins shall not prosper:
but whoso confesseth and forsaketh them shall have mercy.
Proverbs 28:13

A GREAT MAN
IS ALWAYS WILLING
TO BE LITTLE.

~

But the greatest among you shall be your servant.
Matthew 23:11 NASB

AN HONEST MAN'S WORD IS AS GOOD AS HIS BOND.

~

But let your "Yes" be "Yes," and your "No," "No."
James 5:12 NKJV

FIND OUT WHAT YOU LOVE TO DO AND YOU WILL NEVER HAVE TO WORK ANOTHER DAY IN YOUR LIFE.

Stand at the crossroads and look; ask for the ancient paths,
ask where the good way is, and walk in it,
and you will find rest for your souls.
Jeremiah 6:16 NIV

EXPERIENCE IS NOT WHAT HAPPENS TO A MAN, IT'S WHAT A MAN DOES WITH WHAT HAPPENS TO HIM.

~

*For whatever is born of God overcomes the world; and this
is the victory that has overcome the world—our faith.*
I John 5:4 NASB

IT IS THE CHARACTER OF VERY FEW MEN TO HONOR WITHOUT ENVY A FRIEND WHO HAS PROSPERED.

~

A friend loves at all times.
Proverbs 17:17 NRSV

A MAN WHO DOES NOT READ GOOD BOOKS HAS NO ADVANTAGE OVER THE MAN WHO CAN'T READ THEM.

~

Apply thine heart unto instruction,
and thine ears to the words of knowledge.
Proverbs 23:12

NEVER ALLOW YOUR SENSE OF SELF TO BECOME ASSOCIATED WITH YOUR SENSE OF JOB. IF YOUR JOB VANISHES, YOUR SELF DOESN'T.

*What advantage does man have in all his work
Which he does under the sun? A generation goes and
a generation comes, But the earth remains forever.
Ecclesiastes 1:3,4 NASB*

MANY A MAN HAS FOUND THE ACQUISITION OF WEALTH ONLY A CHANGE, NOT AN END, OF MISERIES.

~

He who loves money will not be satisfied with money,
nor he who loves abundance with its income.
Ecclesiastes 5:10 NASB

I AM DEFEATED,
AND KNOW IT, IF I MEET ANY
HUMAN BEING FROM WHOM
I FIND MYSELF UNABLE TO
LEARN ANYTHING.

A wise man will hear, and will increase learning; and a man of understanding shall attain unto wise counsels.
Proverbs 1:5

SHOW ME A MAN WHO CANNOT BOTHER TO DO LITTLE THINGS AND I'LL SHOW YOU A MAN WHO CANNOT BE TRUSTED TO DO BIG THINGS.

You have been faithful and trustworthy over a little;
I will put you in charge of much.
Matthew 25:21 AMP

THE MOST DIFFICULT SECRET FOR A MAN TO KEEP IS THE OPINION HE HAS OF HIMSELF.

~

I warn every one among you...not to have an exaggerated opinion of his own importance; but to rate his ability with sober judgement.
Romans 12:3 AMP

NO ONE EVER SAID ON THEIR DEATHBED: I WISH I WOULD HAVE SPENT MORE TIME AT WORK!

~

Then I considered all that my hands had done
and the toil I had spent in doing it, and again,
all was vanity and a chasing after wind.
Ecclesiastes 2:11 NRSV

THERE IS ONE THING ALONE THAT STANDS THE BRUNT OF LIFE THROUGHOUT ITS LENGTH: A QUIET CONSCIENCE.

~

If our hearts do not condemn us
we have confidence before God.
1 John 3:21 NIV

SHALLOW MEN BELIEVE IN LUCK... STRONG MEN BELIEVE IN CAUSE AND EFFECT.

~

*Be not deceived; God is not mocked: for whatsoever
a man soweth, that shall he also reap.*
Galatians 6:7

DOST THOU LOVE LIFE? THEN DO NOT SQUANDER TIME, FOR THAT IS THE STUFF LIFE IS MADE OF.

Remember how short my time is.
Psalm 89:47

A MAN OF HONOR REGRETS A DISCREDITABLE ACT EVEN WHEN IT HAS WORKED.

~

*A wise man's heart directs him toward the right,
but the foolish man's heart directs him toward the left.*
Ecclesiastes 10:2 NASB

WASTE NO MORE TIME ARGUING WHAT A GOOD MAN SHOULD BE. BE ONE.

~

Be an example (pattern) for the believers, in speech, in conduct, in love, in faith, and in purity.
1 Timothy 4:12 AMP

PROTECT
YOUR OWN CREDIBILITY.
ONE OF THE HIGHEST
ACCOLADES IS THE
COMMENT, "IF HE SAYS SO,
YOU CAN BANK ON IT."

~

Righteous lips are the delight of kings;
and they love him that speaketh right.
Proverbs 16:13

THE MAN WHO IS BORN WITH A TALENT WHICH HE WAS MEANT TO USE FINDS HIS GREATEST HAPPINESS IN USING IT.

*But life is worth nothing unless I use it
for doing the work assigned me by the Lord Jesus.*
Acts 20:24 TLB

A MAN IS NOT FINISHED WHEN HE IS DEFEATED. HE IS FINISHED WHEN HE QUITS.

~

And let us not be weary in well doing:
for in due season we shall reap, if we faint not.
Galatians 6:9

IF A TASK IS ONCE BEGUN,
NEVER LEAVE IT
TILL IT'S DONE.
BE THE LABOR
GREAT OR SMALL,
DO IT WELL OR NOT AT ALL.

~

Whatever your hand finds to do, do it with your might.
Ecclesiastes 9:10 NKJV

GIVE ME A STOCK CLERK WITH A GOAL, AND I WILL GIVE YOU A MAN WHO WILL MAKE HISTORY. GIVE ME A MAN WITHOUT A GOAL AND I WILL GIVE A STOCK CLERK.

...fixing our eyes on Jesus...who for the joy set before Him endured the cross,...and has sat down at the right hand of the throne of God.
Hebrews 12:2 NASB

THE MAN
WHO MAKES NO MISTAKES
DOES NOT NORMALLY
MAKE ANYTHING.

~

Though he fall, he shall not utterly be cast down:
for the Lord upholdeth him with his hand.
Psalm 37:24

REFERENCES

Unless otherwise indicated, all Scripture quotations are taken from the *King James Version* of the Bible.

Scripture quotations marked NIV are taken from the *Holy Bible, New International Version®* NIV®. Copyright © 1973, 1978, 1984 by International Bible Society. Used by permission of Zondervan Publishing House. All rights reserved.

Scripture quotations marked NASB are taken from the *New American Standard Bible*. Copyright © The Lockman Foundation 1960, 1962, 1963, 1968, 1971, 1972, 1973, 1975, 1977. Used by permission.

Verses marked TLB are taken from *The Living Bible*, copyright © 1971. Used by permission of Tyndale House Publishers, Inc., Wheaton, Illinois 60189. All rights reserved.

Scripture quotations marked AMP are taken from *The Amplified Bible, Old Testament* copyright © 1965 by Zondervan Publishing House, Grand Rapids, MI. *New Testament* copyright © 1958 by The Lockman Foundation, La Habra, California. Used by permission.

Scripture quotations marked NRSV are taken from *The New Revised Standard Version Bible*, copyright © 1989 by the Division of Christian Education of the Churches of Christ in the United States of America and is used by permission.

Scripture quotations marked NKJV are taken from *The New King James Version of the Bible*. Copyright © 1979, 1980, 1982, 1994 by Thomas Nelson, Inc., Publishers. Used by permission.

ACKNOWLEDGEMENTS

Elbert Hubbard (6), Robert Shuller (7), Abraham Lincoln (9), A.W. Tozer (10), Dwight L. Moody (11,14,25,44,130), Martin Luther King, Jr. (12), Mark Twain (13,101), Robert Green Ingersol (15), Caroline Fry (17), Thomas Jefferson (18,69), Mike Murdock (19), Paul Tillich (20), Calvin Coolidge (21,46), Frank Crane (22), Cecil G. Osborne (23), David Schwartz (24), James Oliver (27), Anne Bradstreet (28), H.E. Jansen (30), Robert South (32), Margaret Fuller (33), Henry Ward Beecher (34,40), John Wooden (35), James Oppenheim (38), Doris Mortman (41), Richard Exley (43,108), Syrus (45,91), Bill Copland (47), Henry Emerson Fosdick (48), Dr. Eugene Swearingen (49), Ed Cole (50,55), Roy Disney (58), Matthew Prior (59), William A. Ward (60), Moliere (62), Descartes (63), Solon (64), Charles C. Noble (65), Eleanor Roosevelt (66), John Sculley (67), Henry Wadsworth Longfellow (68), Ralph Waldo Emerson (70,132), Charles H. Spurgeon (71), Benjamin Franklin (72), Pauline H. Peters (75), Andrew Jackson (76), Jean Paul Richter (77), William James (78), H.P. Liddon (79), George Elliott (80), John R. Rice (81), Thomas A. Edison (82), George Edward Woodberry (83), Woodrow Wilson (84), William H. Danforth (86), Lillian Dickson (87), Denis Diderot (88), Earl Nightingale (89), Louis D. Brandeis (90), Roy L. Smith (92), Oliver Wendell Holmes (93,104), Albert Einstein (95), Francis Bacon (97), Zig Ziglar (98),

Builder (99), Aristotle (100), George Dana Boardman (102), Gary Smalley & John Trent (103), Arnold H. Glasgow (105), Freeman (106), Doug Larsen (107), Norman Vincent Peale (110), Larry Eisenberg (111), Sir John Buchan (Lord Tweedsmuir) (112), Bern Williams (113), Andrew Carnegie (114), Winston Churchill (120), Jim Patrick (125), Tillotson (126), Billy Graham (127), Parkes Robinson (129), Freidrich Wilhelm Nietzsche (134), James Huxley (135), Aeschylus (136), Gordon van Sauter (138), Lucius Annaeus Seneca (139), George Herbert Palmer (140), Lawrence D. Bell (141), Maurcel Pagnol (142), Euripides (144), H.L. Menken (147), Marcus Aurelius (148), James L. Hayes (149), Richard M. Nixon (151), J.C. Penney (153), Edward John Phelps (154).

Additional Copies of this book and other titles
in the *God's Little Instruction Book* series
are available at your local bookstore.

God's Little Instruction Book

God's Little Instruction Book II

God's Little Instruction Book III

God's Little Instruction Book on Love

God's Little Instruction Book on Prayer

God's Little Instruction Book on Success

God's Little Instruction Book on Character

God's Little Instruction Book for New Believers

*God's Little Instruction Book for Women —
Special Gift Edition*

Honor Books
Tulsa, Oklahoma